BOSS UP

BOSS UP

Written by
Kori Coleman

VMH Publishing

The publisher is not responsible for websites, or social media pages (or their content) related to this publication, that are not owned by the publisher. Quantity sales. Special discounts are available on quantity purchases by corporations, associations, and others.

Paperback ISBN: 979-8-8690-6840-8
E-Book: 979-8-8690-6841-5

Published in United States of America 10 9 8 7 6 5 4 3 2

VMH Publishing
New York, NY - Atlanta, GA

Table of Contents

Preface

I dedicate this book to those who feel lost, misguided, and insecure within themselves. Having walked in your shoes, I understand the struggles you face, and I am still navigating my own journey. Progress is a constant process, and I am here to support you in becoming the person you aspire to be. My motivation comes from personal experiences, conquering challenges, and inspiring others to triumph in any situation.

Throughout my life, I have always been someone who uplifts those around me, so it only seems fitting to extend that motivation to you through this book. As you journey through these pages, it is my sincere hope that you gain valuable insights and empower yourself to boss up in all aspects of life. I offer you tips and guidance to help you reach your highest potential.

Now, when I say "boss up," I am not referring to material possessions, financial prosperity, or relationship status. Bossing up is about elevating your mindset to embrace growth, constantly striving for improvement in every facet of your life. It involves setting healthy boundaries and, above all, living life to the fullest without any regrets.

Life can often feel overwhelming, and it is easy to get caught up in feelings of self-doubt and uncertainty. However, this book aims to provide you with the tools you need to rise above these challenges and embrace a more fulfilling life. It offers practical advice, personal anecdotes, and strategies to overcome obstacles and create the life you desire.

I understand that change can be intimidating, but remember that you are not alone in this journey. Together, we can navigate the complexities of life and find the strength to overcome any obstacles that come our way. So, as you embark on this transformative journey, keep an open mind and allow yourself to grow.

Ready to embark on this journey of self-discovery and empowerment? Let's dive in and begin our quest to boss up and conquer every aspect of our lives!

Introduction

Have you ever experienced that sudden surge of motivation to accomplish something significant in your life, even at the ungodly hour of 3 in the morning? I know, it sounds bizarre, but that's exactly where the inspiration for this book comes from. Its purpose is to help you elevate your mindset and unlock your full potential.

Talking about what you want in life is just the first step, but as you may have already realized, putting those desires into action is easier said than done. I can relate to this struggle all too well. Trying to make positive changes while battling self-doubt and ingrained bad habits can be incredibly challenging. However, the beauty lies in witnessing your personal growth and observing yourself rise to the level you've always envisioned. It's all part of your unique journey that you must learn to embrace wholeheartedly.

The choice is yours - either strive for the life you truly desire or settle for the life that comes your way. Let's face it, everything worth pursuing in life will be difficult, so why not dedicate your efforts to something you are truly passionate about? Forge your own path and create a life that aligns with your values and aspirations.

Now, I must admit that I am still young and may overlook a few aspects, but I am eager to share my knowledge and experiences with you. It is my belief that someone out there is in desperate need of the wisdom and guidance that I can provide. Without further delay, allow me to impart my knowledge and empower you to take control of your life. Let me put you on game...

Chapter 1

Issa Mindset Thing!

It all starts in the mind.

Ever since I graduated from high school, I've been feeling lost, unsure about what my next steps should be and what I truly want from life. My daily routine consisted of going to school, smoking, and hanging out with people who didn't necessarily push me to be my best self. I realized that I was selling myself short and hindering my progress with these bad habits.

One day, I made a decision to change my mindset and actively seek guidance. That's when I stumbled upon a video on YouTube titled "Fixed Mindset vs. Growth Mindset" by Mike Rashid. Little did I know, this video would completely shift my perspective on life. It was then that I heard Funny Marco say, "It's A Mindset Thing." And he couldn't have been more right. Having a growth mindset is the key.

Many people tend to have a "Fixed Mindset," where they believe that their intelligence and beliefs are fixed, often influenced by negative habits or external factors. But the truth is, our minds are powerful tools that should never be wasted. Now, let me tell you about the power of having a growth mindset.

A growth mindset is all about believing in yourself and your ability to achieve anything you set your mind to. People with growth mindsets view failure not as a setback, but as an opportunity to learn and grow. Embracing a growth mindset requires daily practice and resilience. Whenever I face a setback, I no longer see it as a loss, but rather as a lesson that will propel me towards future success. Learning from these lessons and gaining valuable insights are crucial components of a growth mindset.

Over time, dedicating myself to the grind and persevering through challenges will lead me to the fruits of my labor. A growth mindset, filled with positivity, has the power to transform my life and the lives of those around me. I find great joy in inspiring and motivating others, and witnessing my peers succeed brings me immense satisfaction. However, it's important to remember that if there are people who hinder your growth, it's necessary to cut them off. It may be difficult, but that's where true growth begins.

In order to fully embrace a growth mindset, it's crucial to lock in with yourself, fully embrace your personal journey, and take charge of your own growth. Rejecting societal dictates and putting in the effort will lead you down a path filled with excitement and mystery, mostly in your favor.

Personal growth is highly dependent on our individuality and how we navigate the world around us. By putting in deliberate effort, adopting new strategies, and embracing a growth mindset, we can become lifelong learners. While fixed mindsets may offer certain advantages, a growth mindset allows us to explore the richness of life and unlock our true potential, regardless of our circumstances. It's not about one mindset being better than the other; rather, a growth mindset opens doors to the vast possibilities that life has to offer.

So, remember, it all starts in the mind. Embrace a growth mindset, believe in yourself, and watch as your life transforms before your eyes.

Chapter 2

Watch The Company You Keep!

Growing up, I held a naive belief that everyone I encountered was my friend. In my innocence, I went out of my way to assist others, offering them food, shelter, and even extending invitations for sleepovers, under the misguided notion that these acts would earn me their friendship. Little did I know, my expectations were far from reality. Some of these individuals, who I thought were friends, engaged in insidious behaviors behind my back, mocking me, stealing from me, and once, audaciously taking my birthday present on the very day I was meant to enjoy it. At the time, I felt like a fool, but as I reflect upon those experiences now, I find gratitude within myself.

That tumultuous phase in my life taught me a valuable lesson—one that resonates deeply within me to this day. It taught me to be discerning and mindful of the company I keep. There's an adage that aptly captures this sentiment: "Birds of a feather flock together." I firmly believe that the people we surround ourselves with ultimately shape who we become. Sometimes, even if our friends are genuinely good-hearted individuals, the negativity that envelops them can seep into our lives, disrupting our balance. The presence of such negative influences can corrupt even the strongest of moral compasses. One might find themselves unwittingly dragged into illegal activities or influenced to make choices that are antithetical to their personal values. It's important to recognize that a person with nothing to lose often has no qualms about contributing to your loss as well. If it necessitates leading a temporarily solitary life in order to remain aligned with our goals, then we must be willing to make that sacrifice. There's no need to waste our precious time with individuals who lack aspirations and ambition.

It is an unfortunate reality that not everyone who surrounds us has our best interests at heart. Misery, as the saying goes, loves company, and it has the potential to derail our progress. Some people enter our lives with malicious intentions, disguising themselves as our well-wishers. Personally, I attach great importance to the energy that surrounds me.

It's crucial to be astute and gauge the intentions of those we allow into our inner circle. There will be individuals who pretend to uplift us while secretly harboring resentment and disdain. The moment their true colors are unveiled, we must summon the courage to sever ties with them. As TD Jakes sagaciously stated, "Some people need you to be there because they have built a system around your pain." Regrettably, there are those who derive satisfaction from seeing us fall and never recover. These so-called "friends" could very well be enemies in disguise. The presence of such negative vibes around us serves as a barricade against the blessings that life has in store for us. We must firmly and decisively cut them off.

On a more optimistic note, there are individuals who genuinely wish for our success and triumphs! Though they may be scarce, once these special individuals enter our lives, it's essential to hold onto them tightly. Surrounding ourselves with like-minded and driven individuals is enormously beneficial. A friend group that consistently motivates and empowers us, all while holding us accountable, is a rarity worth cherishing. It's important to internalize the fact that not everyone we encounter is meant to accompany us on our life's journey. Some individuals are merely there to impart lessons, helping us grow and evolve. It is crucial to realize that not everyone has our best interests in mind. It's imperative to stick with those who genuinely wish for our prosperity, rather than seek to exploit us for their own gain. Our energy is an invaluable commodity, and not everyone merits access to it. Being in our presence should be seen as a privilege, rather than a given. We mustn't fear solitude, for just as the sun shines brightly in isolation each day, so too can we flourish in our independence.

The betrayals I experienced at the hands of these so-called friends have proved to be invaluable lessons, emphasizing the significance of carefully selecting genuine companions. These painful experiences have led me to establish firm boundaries, prioritizing relationships with individuals who value authenticity and share a mutual commitment to personal growth. Surrounding ourselves with like-minded individuals has the potential to be transformative. When our values and goals align with those around us, a supportive environment is fostered, enabling collective growth. This collective synergy not only fortifies our personal development but also serves as an inspiration to others, encouraging them to pursue their own aspirations amidst life's challenges.

In my quest to surround myself with genuine companions, I have come to realize that the process of finding such individuals requires patience and discernment. It is not enough to simply seek out those who claim to be on a similar path; we must also pay attention to their actions and how they make us feel. Trust is earned, not freely given, and it is important to listen to our gut instincts when it comes to the company we keep.

When we find ourselves in the presence of individuals who bring us joy and support, it is crucial that we reciprocate the same level of care and encouragement. True friendship is built on a foundation of mutual respect and empathy. It is not enough to simply bask in the positive energy they bring to our lives; we must also strive to be a positive force in theirs. Ultimately, the relationships we nurture should be ones that inspire us to become better versions of ourselves, both individually and collectively.

Of course, it is also important to remember that friendships are not infallible. People change, circumstances evolve, and sometimes, even the closest of bonds can be strained. Learning to let go of toxic relationships is just as essential as cultivating healthy ones. Holding onto individuals who bring nothing but negativity into our lives only hinders our personal growth and stunts our potential.

As I have sought to build my inner circle with intention and purpose, I have come to understand the importance of self-reflection and growth as an individual. It is not solely about the company we keep, but also about the energy we radiate and the choices we make. By continuously working on ourselves and striving to be the best version of who we are, we attract like-minded individuals who are on a similar path.

In the end, the chapter of my life filled with misguided friendships and betrayals has served as a valuable lesson in discernment and self-awareness. It has shown me that the company we keep is a reflection of who we are as individuals. By being selective and intentional about the people we allow into our lives, we create an environment conducive to our growth and success. We owe it to ourselves to surround ourselves with those who genuinely support and uplift us, for in their presence, we can truly thrive.

Chapter 3

Everything Is Not What It Seems!

In today's society, many people are often misguided. Personally, I make it a point to constantly preach to my little cousins about the importance of being true to oneself. We live in an era where clout frequently influences people, affecting their morals, mindset, and priorities. Now, clout itself is not necessarily a bad thing; it's the way in which people misuse it that creates problems. Moreover, celebrities too have a significant impact on our society. Some celebrities conduct themselves in a manner that provides opportunities for those less fortunate, while others fail to present a positive image. It can be tempting to believe everything we see, but it is crucial to remember that appearances can be deceiving. Instead, it's always best to remain authentic, as this fosters genuine relationships and ensures trust.

Avoid Gullibility!

The primary purpose of this chapter is to urge you not to be gullible. Remember the age-old adage: if something sounds too good to be true, it probably is. It is essential to maintain a strong and steadfast mind, staying true to your morals and beliefs. Embrace curiosity and seek out the truth for yourself, if it is relevant to your life.

Stay In Your Own Lane!

One of the best things anyone can do is simply be themselves. By staying true to who you are, you can navigate life without being weighed down by the opinions of others. Remember, there is no traffic in your own lane. Embracing your authentic self has the power to inspire others, especially those who may be going through similar experiences as you. While embracing your true self may come with adversity, it is in these moments that resilience is essential. If there are people talking about you, it means that you are standing up for what you believe in, and that is truly remarkable. Instead of comparing yourself to others, recognize that everyone has a unique journey. The most costly mistake one can make is paying attention to the wrong people. Have the courage to stand up for what you believe in, even if you find yourself standing alone.

By championing authenticity and remaining true to ourselves, we can navigate the complexities of today's world with grace and integrity. Remember, appearances can be deceiving, and it's our responsibility to distinguish between what is genuine and what is merely a facade. When we embrace our true selves, we become unstoppable forces, capable of inspiring and uplifting those around us.

True happiness and fulfillment come from embracing our uniqueness and staying true to ourselves. Being authentic doesn't mean being perfect. Embracing our flaws and imperfections is part of being real and accepting ourselves fully. Instead of seeking validation from others, true confidence comes from trusting our instincts and making choices based on our values and beliefs. Authenticity also extends to how we interact with others, being honest and genuine in relationships to build trust and deeper connections. Embracing authenticity may require bravery, but the rewards are worth it. Living authentically attracts like-minded people who appreciate and value us for who we truly are, forming genuine and fulfilling connections. So, let us continue on this journey of self-discovery and authenticity together, knowing that while everything may not be what it seems, we have the power to create our own truth.

Chapter 4

Charge It To The Game!

This is, without a doubt, my favorite chapter in the entire book. The past few years have been filled with experiences that have taught me so much that I feel compelled to write about them. Through countless trials and tribulations, I have managed to persevere and emerge as a wiser and stronger person. The concept of being genuine and experiencing betrayal is something that I still struggle to grasp, but these very experiences have helped shape me into the individual that I am today. Whether it is in friendships, relationships, or within my own family, I have gained valuable insight about not taking things personally and instead, charging it to the game. Allow me to expand on this.

One of the most important things to keep in mind when dealing with people nowadays is to approach situations with a logical mindset rather than letting our emotions dictate our decisions, especially when we feel like we have been played. It's a matter of having mind over matter. We should never allow anyone to trick us out of our position! I understand the feeling of being played, and it often leads us to want to retaliate in one way or another. However, there are times when we simply have to let those individuals miss out on their blessings and prove to them that greater things will always come later. From now on, I focus on teaching my heart to accept disappointment, even from those I love dearly. I have learned that it is much better to allow things to flow naturally instead of forcing them. Life takes a turn for the better when we come to the realization that we don't have to react to every single situation that comes our way. It's important to keep a "playa" mentality and not take things personally. So, let's charge it to the game, rather than charging it to the heart.

But let us not forget, what goes around always comes around. We will always reap what we sow. Just like how a bird eats ants when it's alive, and the ants eat the bird when it dies. It's like how a single match can burn a million trees derived from a single tree. Circumstances change, and time holds more power than we do. Whatever we contribute to the universe will eventually come back to us.

So, it is crucial to do good and be good. By approaching life with a genuine heart and pure intentions, we can trust that things will always end up in our favor. There is no need to jeopardize our future by trying to teach people lessons that the universe will inevitably teach them.

And now, as we navigate the ebb and flow of life together, let us acknowledge the times when we have taken "L's." When I say "L," I don't simply mean a loss, but rather a lesson. Although we may often wish we could rewind time countless times, the show must always go on. Each rejection we face redirects us towards something greater. Life is unpredictable, and we may experience the loss of family, friends, lovers, or even lose ourselves in the process. Yet, some of these losses may actually be blessings in disguise. As Charles R. Swindall once said, "Life is 10% what happens to you and 90% how you react to it." It takes numerous lessons to reach our ultimate destination, but we must always continue learning, pushing ourselves ten times harder, and bouncing back from losses, not lessons.

Life has a way of humbling us and reminding us that we are not invincible. It is in these moments of defeat, these moments that we charge to the game, that we find our true resilience. It is easy to wallow in self-pity and succumb to despair, but that will get us nowhere. Instead, we must rise above the challenges, dust ourselves off, and keep moving forward.

The beauty of charging it to the game is that it allows us to let go of the weight that holds us back. It frees us from dwelling on the past and opens our hearts and minds to new opportunities. It is a mindset shift that allows us to release the burden of disappointment and approach life with a renewed sense of hope and determination.

But let me be clear, charging it to the game does not mean we become passive or complacent. It is not a surrender to the circumstances that have challenged us. No, it is a call to action, a reminder that we have the power to shape our own destiny. It is an invitation to learn from our experiences and use them as fuel to propel us forward.

Charging it to the game requires a certain level of self-awareness and self-reflection. It asks us to confront our own shortcomings and take responsibility for our actions. It pushes us to question our motives and ensure that we are aligned with our true values. It is about being honest with ourselves and recognizing that we, too, have played a role in the game.

As we charge it to the game, let us also remember the importance of forgiveness, both for others and for ourselves. Holding onto grudges only weighs us down and hinders our growth. By forgiving, we release the negative energy that keeps us stuck in the past, and we open ourselves up to the possibilities of a brighter future.

In this journey of charging it to the game, we will inevitably face setbacks and disappointments. But these moments are not defeats; they are merely lessons in disguise. They are opportunities for growth and self-discovery. They are invitations to rise above our circumstances and become the best versions of ourselves.

As we continue on this path, let us embrace the game with open hearts and unwavering determination. Let us charge it to the game and trust that, in doing so, we will not only survive but thrive. Life may knock us down, but we will always get back up, stronger and more resilient than ever before. Charge it to the game and let the adventure continue.

Chapter 5

Calculated Steps!

When it comes to calculated steps, it's important to make your next move your best move. This isn't a game of chess; it's like a game of checkers. However, in order to move forward, you must have a clear understanding of what you want and where you're headed. Instead of waiting for the right time to start, just take that first step.

I still remember the advice my boxing coach gave me 11 years ago: "stay ready so you don't have to get ready, so when it's time to get ready, you're already ready." That lesson has stayed with me all these years. It taught me the value of planning ahead and being prepared. With a solid plan and a growth mindset, there's almost nothing that can stop you! For me, consistency and self-discipline are the keys to success.

When making daily decisions, think about what you're gaining and how it will benefit you. It's okay to have some fun and let loose occasionally, but always remember to make sacrifices for the bigger picture. Giving up temporary enjoyment in order to build long-lasting stability is not a loss. Whether your steps are small or big, make sure they are well-thought-out and will benefit you in the long run.

I used to love sharing my next move with everyone, thinking I would get applause. But in reality, all I received were laughs in my face. I had to learn to be silent because people didn't want to see me succeed; they just wanted to know my game plan. Success doesn't require an audience; it requires focus.

Moving in silence is the best thing you can do for yourself. Life becomes peaceful and smooth when no one knows what you're up to. When you move in silence, people don't know what to attack. Embrace the power of moving in silence and protect your blessings. Not every step in your journey needs to be put in the spotlight. The quietest moves often speak the loudest.

Keep the details of your next move hidden in mystery and let your actions unveil your path.

In a world where not everyone wishes you well, the ability to keep things to yourself becomes a shield. By moving in silence, you build resilience and allow your success to be louder than any whisper from detractors. Sometimes, saying nothing is the wisest thing to do.

Finding the balance between preparedness and adaptability is crucial. It's important to have a solid plan but also remain open to adjustments as unforeseen challenges arise. Having a flexible mindset allows you to navigate these challenges while staying committed to your long-term objectives.

Moving in silence requires resisting the need for external validation. Instead, focus on self-satisfaction and remind yourself of the initial purpose behind your journey. This will help you stay focused on your personal goals without succumbing to the pressure of constant public validation.

Remember, success is not determined by the applause of others, but by the internal satisfaction you feel when you achieve what you set out to accomplish. Trust yourself and your abilities, and let your actions be the proof of your progress.

In a world that seems to thrive on constant updates and oversharing, staying silent about your plans can be a powerful way to protect yourself and your dreams. By keeping your next move hidden, you keep potential detractors at bay and can focus solely on your own growth and success. Take solace in the fact that not every step of your journey needs to be broadcasted to the world. By moving in silence, you remind yourself that the opinions and judgments of others do not define your worth or potential.

Moving in silence also allows you to develop a sense of resilience and adaptability. When unexpected challenges arise, you can adjust your plans without feeling the need to explain or justify every decision to others. Embrace the freedom of being able to pivot and change course as necessary, knowing that your inner compass will guide you towards your ultimate goals.

Remember, it's not about seeking external validation at every turn. Stay focused on the intrinsic value of your journey and the personal growth you are experiencing along the way. By staying true to yourself and your purpose, you can find fulfillment and satisfaction that no amount of public validation can provide.

So, as you move on your path of calculated steps, remember to trust yourself, stay focused on your goals, and move in silence. Embrace the power of quiet determination and let your actions speak louder than any words. With each step forward, you are paving the way towards your own version of success. Keep going, and never underestimate the strength and resilience that lies within you.

Chapter 6

Never Get Too Comfortable!

The biggest mistake you could ever make is getting too comfortable! No matter how successful you are or how comfortable you feel in your relationship, you can never be too sure. We human beings are creatures of change. Sometimes, however, we become complacent and forget what our main goals in life are. Complacency hinders us from changing for the better, and that is something I must admit I struggle with at times.

I find myself getting comfortable by rewarding myself excessively and neglecting my priorities. But now, I work on addressing this issue by asking myself if this is truly what I want out of life. This question helps me realign my focus because there is so much more I aspire to achieve than just indulging in short-term pleasures and materialistic pursuits. So, I urge you to never retreat or surrender, just keep grinding. Embrace discomfort!

To avoid becoming too comfortable, I always keep myself grounded. Planning ahead before each new week helps me with this. When I plan, I prioritize my health, work, improving my skills, giving back to those in need, and spending quality time with loved ones. Doing so brings structure and discipline into my life. I believe that being grounded keeps us connected to reality and helps us maintain humility. It is essential to remain focused on what truly matters and ensure that our actions align with our goals.

I have learned a great deal from successful people through podcasts, and one common trait they all possess is "focus." They do not waste time and never lose sight of the bigger picture. If you know what you want, you have to go and get it. Do not waste your time, and certainly do not let others waste it for you! Maintain focus on the larger goals and aspirations throughout your journey. This focus will enable you to remain resilient, regardless of life's ups and downs, and lead you to your ultimate destination.

It is important to stay aware of your surroundings, but most importantly, your potential. Opportunities do not wait around, and neither should you. Achieving a balance between self-rewards and discipline requires self-discipline. Not every accomplishment needs extravagant celebration; acknowledging your progress can be a powerful motivator in itself. Plan smaller celebrations, like sharing a meal with friends, to recognize achievements while staying focused on long-term goals.

Prioritizing actions that align with your life objectives requires regular reflection on your goals and priorities. Set clear priorities, create a schedule, and consistently remind yourself of the "why" behind your pursuits. This will help maintain clarity and determination in the face of distractions.

Remember, time is valuable, and pursuing your dreams demands action. Thus, in your pursuit of goals, it is crucial to avoid the trap of comfort. Complacency is indeed the enemy of progress. Regardless of how successful or content you may feel, staying focused on your main life goals is essential. The key is to keep grinding, never retreat or surrender. Put all your excuses to the side and get comfortable with being uncomfortable.

Comfort can be tempting. It seduces us into a state of complacency, where we settle for mediocrity and allow our potential to go untapped. But true growth lies in pushing ourselves outside of our comfort zones, embracing discomfort, and constantly challenging ourselves to reach new heights.

As I continue on my own journey, I have come to recognize the danger of becoming too comfortable. It is in those moments of comfort that we stop growing, stop learning, and stop evolving. I have seen too many people fall victim to the allure of comfort, only to wake up one day and realize that they have settled for less than they deserve.

So I challenge you, dear reader, to break free from the shackles of comfort. Do not let yourself be lulled into a false sense of security. Instead, take risks, pursue new opportunities, and step into the unknown. Only by doing so can we discover our true potential and live a life that is truly fulfilling.

In embracing discomfort, we open ourselves up to a world of possibilities. We become more resilient, adaptable, and open-minded. We learn to navigate uncertainty and embrace change. And most importantly, we continue to grow and evolve as individuals.

But embracing discomfort is not always easy. It requires courage, determination, and a willingness to step outside of our comfort zones. It means facing our fears head-on, even when everything inside of us is screaming to stay put. It means taking risks, even when failure is a possibility. And it means pushing ourselves beyond our limits, even when every fiber of our being is telling us to stop.

But the rewards that come from embracing discomfort are immeasurable. We discover new strengths within ourselves, develop resilience in the face of adversity, and unlock a sense of self-empowerment that can only be attained through the pursuit of discomfort.

So I encourage you to never get too comfortable. Embrace the challenges, the uncertainties, and the discomfort that life throws your way. For it is in those moments that you will discover who you truly are and what you are truly capable of. Keep pushing, keep striving, and never settle for anything less than your full potential. Your future self will thank you for it.

Chapter 7

Take Care Of Yourself!

Sometimes, in the midst of chasing our dreams, we forget to take care of ourselves. We become so wrapped up in our goals and aspirations that we neglect to indulge in self-care. However, it's important to remember that as much work as we put in, we also need to reward ourselves. And it doesn't have to be a grand gesture; even the smallest things can make a difference. Treating yourself to a nice meal, enjoying a spa day, or engaging in a hobby you love can be just as meaningful.

In fact, setting aside time for hobbies is another form of self-care and self-rewarding. Beyond the demands of our goals and professional aspirations, these activities provide a sanctuary for peace and joy. Engaging in hobbies is an investment in our own happiness and personal growth. They allow us to express ourselves in a genuine and meaningful way, adding strokes of color to the masterpiece that is our lives.

So remember to treat yourself! Rewards play a crucial role in our brain's chemistry by increasing dopamine levels. Dopamine, a neurotransmitter, not only contributes to feelings of happiness, but also enhances memory retention, aids in sleep, and regulates mood and appetite. By taking a moment to celebrate our victories, whether they're big or small, we empower ourselves and infuse our journey with motivation and resilience. It's not just about reaching our goals; it's about experiencing joy along the way.

Elevate your journey by embracing these moments of self-satisfaction as power moves in self-love. Replenish yourself with the energy and positivity needed to navigate your hustle. Recognize that self-care is a key strategy in your rise to success. It's not just about climbing the ladder; it's about maintaining your higher self mentally and physically. So, treat yourself like the boss you are, recharge your ambition, and stay on top of your game.

In these moments of self-empowerment, you're not just navigating life; you're mastering the art of bossing up and thriving in your narrative of success. On this long journey of chasing our dreams, it's easy to overlook the need for self-love. So, while pursuing our goals, let's not forget to embrace self-rewards, replenish our energy, and maintain our higher selves. Bossing up is about more than just reaching new heights; it's about embracing self-love and excelling in our own story of success.

Creating a balance between self-indulgence and discipline requires setting clear boundaries. It's important to establish healthy limits by understanding our personal thresholds and effectively communicating them. Learning to say "no" when necessary, such as declining requests for financial assistance without a genuine connection, fosters mutual respect. Asserting boundaries and saying "no" has allowed me to regain control over my time and energy. Though it can be difficult, this shift has enabled me to focus on essential tasks, maintain a healthier work-life balance, and contribute positively to my self-respect and overall well-being.

Moreover, prioritizing self-care also means addressing our physical health. Ensuring we get enough sleep, eat nourishing meals, and exercise regularly are all crucial components of maintaining our well-being. It's easy to overlook these basics when we're consumed by our ambitions, but without a strong foundation of good health, our journey becomes much more challenging.

Remember, taking care of ourselves is not a selfish act. In fact, it allows us to show up fully for our dreams and those around us. When we neglect our own needs, we risk burning out and losing sight of why we started in the first place. It's important to cultivate a mindset of self-compassion and understand that fueling our own happiness is not only beneficial for ourselves but for everyone else who relies on us.

So, as you continue to chase your dreams with unwavering determination, don't forget to take a step back every now and then. Take a deep breath, indulge in a moment of self-care, and remind yourself of the incredible journey you're on. By nourishing your mind, body, and soul, you're not only ensuring your own success but creating a ripple effect of inspiration and motivation for others.

Self-care is not a luxury; it's a necessity. It's a vital aspect of our journey towards success and fulfillment. So, don't forget to celebrate your wins, engage in activities that bring you joy, and prioritize your well-being. By doing so, you'll not only reach your goals but also become the best version of yourself. Keep hustling, keep growing, and remember to always take care of yourself along the way.

Chapter 8

Stand On Business!

I used to tolerate a lot because I didn't want to lose people. Now, I establish boundaries because I don't want to lose myself. Your boundaries are your keepers and protectors. Train them to outshine your gentle heart, empowering your mind to triumph over emotions. By refusing to tolerate disrespect, you prioritize self-care. Remember, stepping away from tables lacking respect is a bold act of nurturing your own growth and well-being. Boundaries are never about telling others what they can and cannot do. They are about telling people what you will and will not accept. Setting healthy boundaries is important.

While kindness is valuable, being overly accommodating can be detrimental. Prioritize self-care and ensure that your kindness doesn't lead to your own detriment. Stand On Your Word! In life, keeping your word is crucial. It's not just about saying something;

it's about living by it. If you make a promise or take a stand, stand firm on it. Let your actions back up your words. Practicing what you preach means aligning your beliefs with your behaviors. It's like a pledge to consistency, building trust by being true to your principles day in and day out. Think of authenticity as your superpower. It's not just a nice quality; it's a force that empowers and earns respect. Rise above the temptation to talk the talk without walking the walk. Your authenticity is a song that others can hear and be inspired by. So, in the journey of life, stand by your words, let your actions reflect your beliefs, and create a legacy built on honesty and consistency.

Say No! Embracing the power of saying 'no' is like opening a door to self-respect and reclaiming control over your time and energy. You can't let yourself loose trying to please everybody. You have a big heart? I do too, but at some point, you have to put that foot down and let them know, this ain't that. It's a powerful tool for maintaining balance in your life and preventing burnout. Remember, prioritizing yourself is not selfish; it's an act of self-care. You can still be a good person and say no! If they can't respect that, cut them off. If someone can't accept a no, they are a leech, point blank, period. Stand firm, let your 'no' echo, and watch as the leeches fade away, leaving space for the crescendo of your self-care and well-being.

In the evolution of self-discovery, I've shifted from tolerating too much for fear of losing others to establishing boundaries that safeguard my essence. Your boundaries are your fortress, keepers and protectors of your authenticity. Train them to outshine your gentle heart, empowering your mind to triumph over emotions. Refusing disrespect isn't just about setting limits; it's a commitment to self-care.

Keeping your word isn't just a principle; it's a pact to live authentically. Align beliefs with actions, pledging consistency that builds trust day by day. Drawing the line between accommodation and healthy boundaries involves listening to one's intuition. Establishing predetermined goals and planning for modest celebrations help strike a balance between acknowledging successes and staying disciplined. Consistently setting aside time for self-reward and rejuvenation is achieved through scheduling. Planning specific days for self-prioritization ensures a regular commitment to self-care while staying focused on long-term goals.

Authenticity is your superpower, a force that empowers and commands respect. Stand by your words, let your actions reflect your beliefs, and craft a legacy founded on honesty and consistency. Don't let these folks play with you, stand on business!

Maintaining your self-respect and taking control of your time and energy requires embracing the power of saying 'no'. It's not about being selfish, but about prioritizing yourself and practicing self-care. You have a big heart, and so do I, but there comes a time when you have to draw a line and let others know that certain things are not acceptable. This is a powerful tool for maintaining balance in your life and preventing burnout.

If someone cannot accept your 'no' or respect your boundaries, it's important to recognize them as a leech. Cut them off and stand firm in your decision. By doing so, you create space for the crescendo of your self-care and well-being. Allow your 'no' to echo and watch as these individuals fade away, leaving you with peace and freedom.

In the journey of self-discovery, I've shifted from fearing the loss of others to valuing my own essence by establishing boundaries. These boundaries serve as my fortress, protecting and nurturing my authenticity. Through training them to outshine my gentle heart, I empower my mind to triumph over emotions and refuse disrespect.

Living authentically goes beyond merely talking about your beliefs; it requires embodying them through consistent actions. Let your authenticity shine like a song that others can hear and be inspired by. Rise above the temptation to just talk the talk and make a pledge to consistently walk the walk. This commitment to authenticity will not only empower yourself but also earn the respect and admiration of those around you.

As you continue on your journey, remember to stand on your business! Establish healthy boundaries and prioritize your self-care. Say 'no' when necessary and let your actions reflect your beliefs. With each step you take, you are building a legacy of honesty, consistency, and authenticity. Embrace the power within you and watch as your life transforms into a reflection of your true self.

Chapter 9

YOLO!

ook, we only have one life to live, so why not make the most of every aspect of it? Your potential knows no bounds. You have the remarkable ability to manifest anything your mind sets its focus on. Imagine the vastness of the sky; that's the expanse of possibilities awaiting your touch. The essence of success lies in embracing the belief that turning dreams into reality is not just an aspiration but an achievable reality.

As you embark on this journey, always remember that the sky is not the limit; it's merely the beginning of the limitless potential you carry within. Anything is possible when fueled by passion, determination, and a steadfast commitment to transforming aspirations into tangible achievements. So, dream boldly, pursue relentlessly, and let the vastness of your potential be the guiding force in crafting a future where the impossible becomes nothing more than a stepping stone to the extraordinary.

But don't let the pursuit of success blind you to the joy and beauty of everyday life. Love your life. Take a moment to express your love to your family, engage in activities that genuinely bring you joy and happiness. There is so much in this world to live for, and it's up to you to go out and explore, to discover what truly resonates with your soul. Live your life like it's your last day because, if you don't, you'll only regret the chances you didn't take.

Surround yourself with positive influences that uplift your spirit and inspire you to become the best version of yourself. Cultivate gratitude for the small moments, for they are the building blocks of a fulfilling journey. And remember, every challenge that comes your way is an opportunity for growth. Your resilience will shape a remarkable story that testifies to your strength and determination.

To fully embrace the richness of life, not only live with intention but also savor the present moment. Each day is an opportunity to create a masterpiece of purpose and fulfillment. Life is a journey filled with opportunities to savor, explore, and create unforgettable memories. Learn to love yourself for who you truly are, embracing your authenticity and celebrating your unique qualities. Embrace the evolution into the person you're becoming, even if it means facing potential resistance from others.

Some may not like the changes you're making, but don't let that discourage you. Keep pushing forward and bossing up, because your happiness is what truly matters. It's important to understand the difference between happiness and contentment. While contentment can lead to complacency, happiness fuels your spirit and keeps you motivated to reach for greater heights. Surround yourself with those who uplift your spirit and add joy to your journey, for they will be your pillars of support.

Always remember that life's beauty lies not just in reaching a destination but also in the joyous, unpredictable dance of the journey itself. Embracing authenticity in the face of potential resistance requires self-reflection and a commitment to personal growth. I have personally overcome the challenge of not having a role model, and in doing so, I have learned to be the person I aspire to become. I have embraced my uniqueness and evolved authentically.

Distinguishing between happiness and contentment requires a proactive approach. By setting goals, seeking meaningful experiences, and staying adaptable, you can prevent complacency from taking hold. It's essential to strike a balance between contentment and an ongoing pursuit of happiness, ensuring a dynamic and fulfilling life journey.

As you navigate the complexities of life, remember that you hold so much power within you. You have the ability to create a life that is truly extraordinary. Dream big, pursue your passions, and don't be afraid to take risks. Embrace your authenticity, and don't be discouraged by those who may not understand your journey. Stay true to yourself, stay resilient, and always know that the journey itself is what truly matters.

In the pursuit of personal growth, it is essential to constantly challenge yourself and step outside of comfort zones. Taking risks and pushing boundaries allows for personal development and the discovery of hidden strengths and passions. Embracing the unknown and being open to new experiences will only enhance your journey and lead to greater fulfillment.

It is crucial to surround yourself with positive and supportive influences. The people you choose to have in your life can greatly impact your mindset, motivation, and overall well-being. Seek out individuals who believe in your potential and push you to be the best version of yourself. Together, you can inspire each other to achieve greatness and overcome any obstacles that may arise.

While it is important to set goals and strive for success, it is equally important to find joy in the present moment. Appreciating the small victories and celebrating progress along the way can create a sense of fulfillment and motivation to continue on the path. Life is a delicate balance between planning for the future and cherishing the present, and finding that balance will lead to a more meaningful and purposeful existence.

In the process of self-discovery and personal growth, you may encounter resistance from others who may not fully understand or support your journey. It is important to remember that the opinions of others do not define your worth or potential. Stay true to yourself, embrace your uniqueness, and continue to evolve authentically. Remember, the most extraordinary individuals often face the most resistance. Embrace the challenge and use it as fuel to drive your aspirations forward.

Life is a precious gift, and you only have one chance to make the most of it. Embrace the vastness of possibilities that lie before you, and let your potential guide you towards a fulfilling and purpose-driven existence. Love fiercely, appreciate the journey, and never be afraid to embrace your authentic self. The possibilities are endless when you dare to dream boldly and live each day with intention.

Conclusion

As I reflect on the experiences that compelled me to write this book, I am reminded of the incredible highs and challenging lows that have shaped my journey. It is with great purpose that I sought to share the invaluable lessons I have learned along the way, for I believe they can bring value and inspiration to those in search of personal growth.

As we arrive at the conclusion of this book, my deepest hope is that it has provided you with profound insights on how to embrace your true self and become the best version of yourself, solely for your own sake. Remember, this is your life, and you possess the power to take charge of it. Engage in activities that bring you inner peace and genuine happiness, while also actively contributing something meaningful to your personal journey.

Never forget to passionately pursue what you love, spread love to others, revel in your unique qualities, and dance joyously in the realization of your authentic self. And when faced with critics or those who seek to bring you down, always remember that their words hold no true power over you. In fact, their chatter may very well be an indication that you are on the right path, making significant strides toward greatness!

As I bring this book to a close, I encourage you to let these lessons and words serve as a guiding light of motivation in your own life. Embrace each experience, both the triumphant moments and the trying times, as stepping stones on your beautifully unique journey. Your path, dear reader, is a masterpiece in the making, and with every step you take, you are composing a symphony that resonates with purpose and fulfillment. So let it play loudly and proudly, for as Luke 1:37 reminds us, "For nothing will be impossible with God."

May you carry these truths in your heart, and may they inspire you to live a life filled with unyielding passion, unwavering authenticity, and limitless possibilities. You have the power within you to create a future where dreams become reality, and I have no doubt that you will leave an indelible mark upon this world.